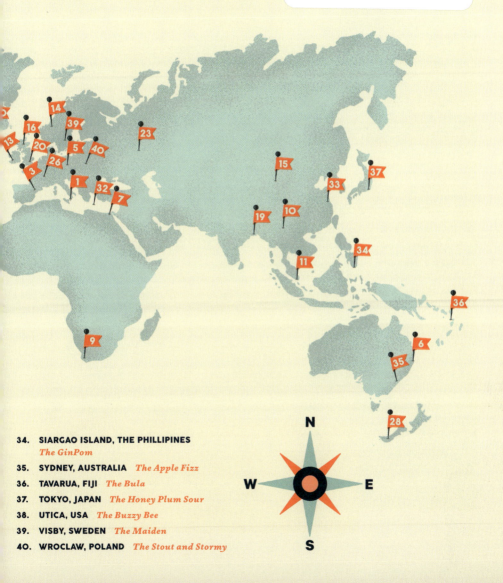

World COCKTAIL · ADVENTURES ·

Hardie Grant

EXPLORE

CONTENTS

INTRODUCTION

Welcome all travel and cocktail enthusiasts! Perhaps you bought this book to improve your mixology skills or to learn about far-flung locations around the world. Or perhaps you received this book as a gift from your uncle who clearly knows nothing about you. Whatever the case may be, we are glad to have you here. We hope you learn a thing or two, or maybe pick up a trick to share with friends ... but at the very least, we hope you enjoy all the purdy pictures.

With such a vast and intriguing world, there is so much to explore. This book is for those who like the thrill and mystery of the unknown—or anyone willing to take a trip of the mind in lieu of actual traveling. This is our attempt to make even the most far-off and exotic locations feel familiar.

Traveling and cocktails are integral parts of The Whiskey Ginger brand—whiskey is right there in our name, see? Our work is inspired by the people we meet while traveling—their stories, ideas, and unique perspectives. We've learned that the best things can be found in the strangest of places, hidden in the nooks and crannies of a vast world. Traveling helps us ignite the creative spark, and the sights and sounds of a new location really are best experienced with a drink in hand.

And now, we're asking you to come on an adventure with us ... a cocktail adventure ... you know ... like the book's title. This book is recreational romanticism. When writing about something fun, like traveling and cocktails, we thought it was important to approach each destination with matching levity.

We aim to create a sense of time and place for you to get lost in (and not just because you sampled seventeen recipes in a row): adventure, delight in indulgence, and the joy of discovery. The style is a nod to iconic travel poster art, with a touch of modern flair. We hope to evoke the spirit of a destination—even a romanticized version—as best we can.

This book is meant to be used. It's not your mom's white couch. Dust jackets be gone. Write in it. Spill a drink on it. Pass it around. Love was poured into the making of it, and you can honor the creators by truly enjoying it. Cheers!

ABOUT THE CREATORS

This book was illustrated and written by Loni Carr and Brett Gramse. Together, we are the creators behind The Whiskey Ginger, a design brand based out of the beautiful mountain town of Bozeman, Montana. Loni Carr is the illustrator and artist extraordinaire whose lovely work can be seen throughout the pages of this book. Brett Gramse is the "writer" whose words fill up the less beautiful parts of the book.

Our creative process is a nod to simpler times: a pre-digital age, when people could connect face to face, collaborate, and share the wildest of ideas until they started to sound sane. With many late nights in the design studio, whiskey has become our unofficial muse, warming our hearts and fueling our drive. We've found that a good cocktail is the best lubricant for the generation of ideas. That's why we feel the name of our business, The Whiskey Ginger, is so fitting. It's about the quest for that superlative spirit; take out the creative endeavor, and you've still got something to sip on.

When it comes to coherent design, visuals are strengthened by quality copy, and vice-versa. As a design and copy team, we do our best to interpret and bring to life even the most obscure of notions. We share this inspiration through a variety of mediums. We draw, we play music, we sing, we take pictures, and we write—all in the hopes of capturing those ever-elusive idiosyncrasies that a passing glance might overlook.

We rub elbows with cowboys and up-start entrepreneurs alike. We pass time in the company of wayward ski bums as often as those with a bit more blue in their blood. We feel at home drinking bottom-shelf whiskey and PBR in dim-light dives, but we also like drinking espresso martinis for $20 a pop in trendy-chic bars. Our parents have suggested that maybe we should spend less time in bars ... but IT'S PART OF THE BRAND, MOM!

Having abandoned the 9–5 mentality long ago, we live in a world of our own design while the constant threat of idleness nips at our heels. The repercussions of working for ourselves tend to pop up in the strangest of places, but we wouldn't trade it for the world. We'll continue to throw our heads against the wall looking for a way through. And that's fine by us.

We've traveled thousands of miles together, and we always bring our dogs with us. There's Gwenny the mini Aussie and Winter, a feral Great Pyrenees mix. They are our trusted allies and favorite traveling companions. We're all travelers at heart.

If you care to find out more about The Whiskey Ginger brand, feel free to reach out to us through our website: whiskeyginger.com. Or if you're feeling spendy, check out some of our merchandise on Society6, Etsy (WhiskeyGingerDesign), or elsewhere on the interwebs. Cheers!

THIS WAY FOR

Adventures & RECIPES

REYKJAVÍK

~ Iceland ~

Iceland's name supposedly comes from a Viking named Hrafna-Flóki, who scaled a tall mountain and spotted an iceberg floating—as icebergs tend to do—in the sea below. Apparently, this occasion was so incredibly momentous that an entire country deemed it an acceptable namesake. I guess "obvious observation land" didn't have the same ring to it.

The name "Iceland" stuck, despite the fact that Iceland is famously greener than Greenland. Perhaps those early Icelanders were doing their best to dissuade any new settlers from trying their luck in this lovely new country.

And can you blame them?

Over the years, Iceland has become known as "the land of ice and fire" due to its many glaciers, hot springs, geysers, and volcanoes. The ice and fire juxtaposition is also useful in describing Reykjavík, Iceland's largest city and capital. How, you ask? Well, I'll tell you: Reykjavík is the world's northernmost capital city (ice) and the nightlife in this city of roughly 130,000 is simply fire. There, I've made a perfectly legitimate comparison. (For all ye olde folks out there, calling something "fire" is praise, roughly equivalent to saying something is really good.) And Reykjavík's nightlife IS really good—legendary, in fact. Tourists flock to the city from all over the world to get a taste of Iceland's singular after-hours entertainment.

> **FUN FACT:** *Iceland has a notoriously small genealogical pool, so if you plan to go to Iceland in search of your one true love, not being someone's distant cousin could play out in your favor. (No promises.)*

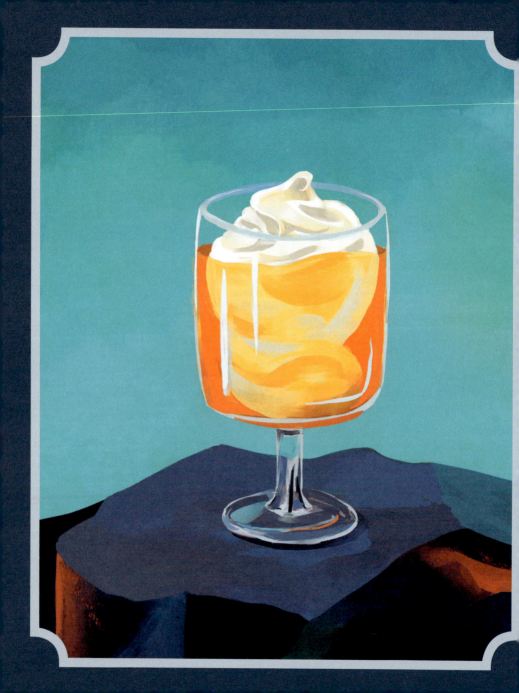

FIRE and ICE

In a land of ice and fire, let's mix a drink to match. Say hello to the Fire and Ice: a delicious mix of cinnamon whiskey, vanilla ice cream, and other ingredients to help cool your burning desires.

SERVES 1

drizzle of caramel sauce

2 small scoops of vanilla ice cream

2 oz (60 ml) cinnamon whiskey

2 oz (60 ml) cream soda

Drizzle the caramel sauce into a highball glass to decorate. Add the vanilla ice cream, then pour in your cinnamon whiskey, and top with the cream soda.

NOTE: *You could try replacing the whiskey with Brennivín, Iceland's signature liquor, also called "Black Death." The flavor is described as black licorice, caraway, and cumin (yum?). Not quite "fire," but it could work if you're feeling adventurous.*

CUSCO

~ Peru ~

Cusco, Peru, was once the capital of the massive Inca empire and is the oldest continuously inhabited city in the Americas. Many of the stone structures built during Incan times can still be seen today, and Cusco's historical importance led to it being listed as a UNESCO World Heritage Site in 1983.

Aside from being whizzes with stone construction, the Inca were also among the first to ferment alcohol for consumption. Chicha—a corn-based beer—dates back to roughly 5000 BCE and is still enjoyed today. With such a long history of drinking, the Peruvians surely know a thing or two about having a good time.

So if you plan to head to this beautiful and historic city, brush up on your Spanish and get ready to immerse yourself in an exciting and thriving culture full of friendly and welcoming people.

Maybe you're headed to Peru on vacation ... or maybe you're trying to escape your intolerable children or other vexatious worldly obligations.

Whatever the case may be, the friendly folks of Peru will welcome you with open arms (unless you're a real jerk).

Blood Orange
PISCO SOUR

Pisco is a brandy distilled from grapes, originating back in the 16th century. Both Chile and Peru claim pisco as their own creation, and it's a source of heated dispute still today. The Pisco Sour cocktail is equally controversial, with both Chile and Peru flaunting their own variation as the original drink. Can't we all just make a drink or three and get along? Here, we offer the Peruvian version (with egg whites) with the addition of blood orange (to sweeten that bad blood). Now sip and make up.

SERVES 2

4 oz (125 ml) pisco

4 oz (125 ml) blood orange
 juice

2 egg whites

crushed ice

Angostura bitters

blood orange slices,
 to garnish

 Add the pisco, blood orange juice, and egg white to a cocktail shaker. Shake vigorously for 60 seconds. Add the crushed ice to the shaker and shake another 60 seconds. Strain into two coupe glasses and top with a few drops of bitters and a blood orange slice garnish. If you can't find blood orange juice or fresh blood oranges, plain oranges or orange juice will do fine.

NOTE: *Consuming raw egg white may increase your risk of foodborne illness. For us, we like to live a little.*

QUEENSTOWN
~ Aotearoa New Zealand ~

Queenstown, Aotearoa New Zealand, aptly dubbed "the adventure capital of the world", is the *perfect* place to satisfy your thrill-seeking side. Bungee jumping, hang-gliding, zip lining—if it's an adrenaline-pumping good time you're after, the Kiwis in Queenstown have got your fix.

It's worth mentioning that extreme sports and alcohol *DON'T MIX*. Wait until *after* your bungee jump to have a drink, you animal.

If team sports are more up your alley, consider checking out an All Blacks rugby match. Aotearoa New Zealand's national rugby team typically play their home games at Eden Park in Auckland, but the team is so beloved that most bars in the country will be playing the game live on TV. It's an event more amenable to consuming a few adult beverages anyway—in fact, watching an All Blacks match and *not* having a drink or two might raise suspicion. And if you find yourself in a pub looking for some stats to throw out there to prove your fandom, here's one for ya: the All Blacks are the most successful international rugby team of all time, boasting a 77 percent winning percentage over the course of their 100-plus-year history. That's something worthy of celebrating with the friends you're sure to make at the bar! New Zealanders will be the first to tell you: good times are made more gooder with the help of a cocktail or two.

The
KIWI DAREDEVIL

When you're in the adventure capital of the world, why not throw caution to the wind and mix up something to thrill the soul? The Kiwi Daredevil will test your mettle and help make the most of any moment.

SERVES 1

2 kiwis, peeled and sliced

1.5 oz (45 ml) freshly squeezed lime juice

3 fresh mint leaves

1 basil leaf

1 oz (30 ml) agave nectar or pineapple juice

2 oz (60 ml) blanco tequila

crushed ice

In a cocktail shaker, gently muddle most of your kiwi (reserving one slice for garnish), the lime juice, herbs, and agave nectar.

Add your tequila and crushed ice and shake vigorously as you count to ten (or whatever number you are capable of counting to).

Pour (do not strain) your cocktail into a chilled collins glass and garnish with the extra kiwi slice.

NOTE: *This recipe is a take on a traditional smash. Fun note—you can mix up your smash game as long as you stick to four main ingredients: a spirit, a fruit, a sweetener, and herbs (traditionally mint plus another complementary herb).*

NASHVILLE

~ Tennessee, USA ~

Nashville and country music go together like a cowboy hat and dusty boots. Something about the air down in the land of Dixie seems to attract troubadours with a taste for twang. That's not to say Nashville is *only* about country music—there are plenty of up-and-coming bands that would scoff at a request to hear a Garth Brooks cover—but the beating heart of the city still pumps like a fretless bass line behind a three-chord song about lost love ... or drinking ... or heavy-drinking lost loves.

So if you find yourself wanting to live out that country outlaw fantasy, simply roll your rusty truck into town with a guitar, your favorite pair of well-worn jeans, and a six-pack of cold American lager. A tattoo of an eagle carrying the American flag is optional but will only earn you more points. Go ahead and play the part—surely this town needs at least *one* more rebel romantic looking for stardom.

The HIGH NOTE

The sweltering heat of summer in the American south is hard to endure without the help of a refreshingly cold cocktail. This Dixieland delight delivers some sweet southern comfort that'll leave your taste buds on a ... *high note*.

HIGH NOTE FOR ONE

2 oz (60 ml) whiskey

1 oz (30 ml) peach schnapps

4 oz (120 ml) sweet tea (store-bought or homemade)

1 lemon slice

1 peach slice

1 sprig of mint

HIGH NOTE FOR 4

2 cups whiskey

1 cup peach schnapps

4 cups sweet tea (store-bought or homemade)

1 lemon, sliced

1 peach, sliced

4 sprigs of mint

 Combine everything in a cold pint glass or pitcher with plenty of ice. Sip slowly with a smile.

UTICA

~ *Montana, USA* ~

Montana: a state synonymous with adventure, romanticism, and rugged individualism. This large state in the northwestern U.S. has plenty to offer anyone who finds themself there: majestic mountains, endless rivers, wildlife, and scenic beauty everywhere you look. People from all walks of life—from dusty cowboys to startup entrepreneurs—call Montana home.

With such an eclectic group, it's hard to find a common thread among them. But certainly *one* common thread is a penchant for drinking. Not everyone who lives there is a drinker, of course, but stay long enough, and you just might become one. Why, you ask? Maybe it's due to all the top-notch craft breweries and distilleries pumping out delicious brews and spirits like they're going out of style (they ain't). Or perhaps it's the cold winters or the constant threat of a grizzly bear attack that drives Montanans to drink. Whatever the reason—and there are *many*—Montana has earned a reputation as a sanctuary for drinkin' folk.

Utica is a small, unincorporated community smack dab in the middle of Montana—a perfect launching place to embark on all sorts of outdoor adventures and experience the state much like it was a century ago.

The
BUZZY BEE

Let's make like a bee and get *buzzed* ... because the name of this cocktail is The Buzzy Bee and it was just TOO tempting not to use the perfectly obvious pun. Montanans love puns.

SERVES 1

2 oz (60 ml) bourbon

1 oz (30 ml) lemon juice

1 oz (30 ml) lavender-honey simple syrup

lemon swath

splash of soda water

LAVENDER-HONEY SIMPLE SYRUP

1 cup water

1 tablespoon dried lavender

½ cup clover honey

To make the lavender-honey simple syrup, bring the water to a boil in a small saucepan over a medium heat. Remove from the heat and stir in the lavender and honey until the honey dissolves. Let sit for 30 minutes. Strain out the lavender with a fine-mesh sieve, and transfer the syrup to an airtight container. It will keep in the fridge for up to 2 weeks.

To assemble the cocktail, combine the bourbon, lemon juice, and lavender-honey simple syrup in a cocktail shaker and shake.

Strain over small ice cubes into a collins glass with a lemon swath. Top with a splash of soda.

NOTE: *You can find delicious premade lavender-honey simple syrups at many craft liquor stores or even online shops, but if you'd like to make your own, be sure to purchase culinary-grade lavender—often found in the herb section at the grocery store.*

SANTORINI

~ Greece ~

Greece is a land synonymous with beautiful weather, romantic getaways, ancient myths, and, of course, delicious cuisine. The island of Santorini is part of the Cyclades islands in the Aegean Sea, distinctive for its quaint white houses sitting atop cliffs overlooking the sea. Santorini was also the site of one of the largest volcanic eruptions in recorded history: the Minoan eruption that devastated the island around 1600 BCE.

There is a lot of culture in Greece. There is also a lot of culture in Greek yogurt. Greek yogurt is a wonderful treat; visiting Greece is a wonderful treat. The comparisons are endless and we could go on, but our editor insisted we don't. Delicious food and drinks on an island in the Aegean Sea? Shouldn't really take convincing for you to visit.

Our advice: load up a flask with some ouzo, and take a trip to the Church of Panagia Episkopi. This thing was built in the 14th century and is still standing. Meanwhile, the birdhouse I built two weeks ago is already broken. Just saying. And once you're ready to move on from your ouzo, drink from "Poseidon's Cup" to keep your Greek adventure running on all cylinders.

POSEIDON'S CUP

Anyone who's been fortunate enough to dip their toes in the beautiful Mediterranean waters of Greece knows the go-to drink is ouzo and water. Ouzo is an anise-flavored liqueur produced and praised in Greece. So why not name our version after the infamous Greek god who controlled the oceans and storms? Let's just leave out the trident-wielding violent temper and sip from our cup with a powerful smile.

SERVES 1

1 large ice cube

2 oz (60 ml) ouzo

3 oz (90 ml) cold water

lemon slice, to garnish

In a rocks glass, place the large cube of quality ice. Pour your ouzo over the ice. As the ouzo's anise reacts with the ice, the spirit will change from transparent to cloudy. Add a splash of very cold water on top. Or, if you really want a drink to put god-like hair on your chest ... skip the ice altogether.

LONDON

~ England ~

Engand is one of the many countries around the world that take their football (or *soccer* to ignorant Americans) *very* seriously. Not as seriously as their tea, mind you, but pretty darn seriously nonetheless.

If you're looking to get rowdy, an English football match is a hell of a place to start. We suggest heading to the nearest pub to watch the game in the company of some avid locals. Who knows, you may even make friends with a true footy hooligan who converts you to a lifelong fan!

And if it's a spirit you need to get prepped for the game, opt for dry gin—a spirit made famous in London during the "Gin Craze" of the early 18th century. During its peak, in the 1730s and '40s, one in every four London households was making gin. On its surface, this sounds like a golden age of drinking, but the reality was that much of what was being produced was of poor quality, and occasionally even deadly. Apparently all those amateur gin distillers weren't quite making top-shelf booze—color me surprised! In an effort to restrict the production and consumption of dangerous liquors, the British government passed the Gin Act of 1751, and consumption began to trail off soon thereafter. (Leave it to the government to put the kibosh on a good time, amirite?) Today the smooth and versatile flavor of London dry gin has become known the world over, with dry gins lacking the sweetness and flavorings typically associated with non-dry gins. One thing is clear: The Brits like their humor like they like their gin – dry.

The HOOLIGAN

As any self-respecting British football fan will tell you, "the beautiful game" is played on a *pitch*, not a *field*. So in honor of the football *pitch*, here's a *pitch*er-full of activities to keep you going strong all day long.

SERVES 6

2 cups London dry gin

¾ cup lime cordial (sweetened lime juice)

1 thinly sliced cucumber, to garnish

1 lime for zesting

splash of soda water (optional)

 Combine the gin and cordial in a pitcher with plenty of ice. Stir vigorously.

Prepare 6 rocks glasses with ice, and pour a serving into each.

Garnish with cucumber slices (for hydration, of course) and zest your lime over each drink. If you like it fizzy, top with a splash of soda water.

TAVARUA

~ Fiji ~

Presumably everyone on earth, at one time or another, has had that life-crisis type of moment that urges them to give it all up and leave for greener pastures ... or sandier beaches.

It's a familiar epiphany that hits like a ton of bricks—a "screw it all" moment that appears when things simply couldn't get any worse. A feeling many Fijians may be familiar with, as Fiji is on the forefront of the battle against climate change.

If you find yourself in need of an escape, why not ride the waves to Tavarua, Fiji, where you'll find plenty of white-sand beaches and friendly folks to help you make that dreamed-of new start.

Tavarua is a small island only a couple miles off Fiji's main island, Viti Levu. With a handful of legendary breaks nearby, this island has cemented its reputation as one of the best surf destinations in the world. But be forewarned: Tavarua's surf breaks are not for the idle dreamer. With strong barreling waves often breaking over shallow and jagged coral reefs, there is little room for error. But for skilled surfers, this is the kind of place that separates the good from the great.

The BULA

When fresh and tangy passion fruits are bountiful, say *Bula* to this cocktail. This deliciously refreshing passion fruit–infused cocktail will make you feel like you're sitting on a white-sand Fijian beach, studiously ignoring all the problems of the world. For this recipe, we substitute passion fruit juice for convenience—but if you're able to locate a fresh passion fruit and juice it, even better.

SERVES 1

small splash of blue Curaçao

2 oz (60 ml) light rum

4 oz (120 ml) passion fruit juice (see Note)

2 sprigs of fresh Thai basil

 Place 1 ice cube in a highball glass and cover with a splash of blue Curaçao.

Separately, in a cocktail shaker, combine rum, passion fruit juice, one spring of Thai basil, and ice.

Shake for about 10 seconds until the mixture is foamy.

Carefully strain the mixture over your prepared glass to create a layered effect, and garnish with the remaining sprig of basil.

NOTE: *To make passion fruit juice, strain the pulp from ripe passion fruits through a mesh strainer, using the back of a spoon to force the juice through and the leaving the seeds behind.*

CHIANG MAI

~ Thailand ~

They call Thailand "the land of a thousand smiles," which is weird since it has a population of around 70 million. I think "The Land of 69,999,000 Frowns" sounds more impressive, but that's just me. While you could spend your holiday counting smiles, I'd suggest you focus on Thailand's beautiful beaches, rich culture, and delicious food. They'd also likely mention the temples of Chiang Mai's Old City, some of which date all the way back to the city's founding in 1296. Temples like Wat Phra Singh, Wat Chedi Luang, Wat Phan Tao, and Wat Chiang Man feature beautifully ornate architecture and are among the most popular attractions in Chiang Mai's Old City. As an added bonus, it's easy to walk between each temple on foot, so you can bone up on the city's history at your own chosen speed.

Another thing Chiang Mai has going for it is its relatively cheap cost of living. Your biggest expense, as is often the case, will be getting here. Once you've arrived, it won't cost an arm and a leg for accommodations, dining, or getting around town. With so much to do and see—even on a shoestring budget—it's no wonder that roughly 10 million people visit Chiang Mai every year. So there's no excuse to not sample all the distinct tastes and flavors of the region.

One of which is the inspiration for Thailand's cocktail: The Toasted Coconut.

The TOASTED COCONUT

CHIANG MAI, THAILAND

This endlessly alluring coconut concoction never disappoints ... so if you find yourself in "the land of a thousand smiles," turn that frown upside down with this toasted coconut delight!

SERVES 1

raw coconut flakes to rim the glass

2 oz (60 ml) light rum

½ oz (15 ml) banana liqueur

juice of ½ lime

2 oz (60 ml) cream of coconut, plus extra for the rim

lime wedge, to garnish

Toasting raw coconut flakes adds a special nutty-sweet crunch before each delicious sip. Place the coconut in a dry skillet over a medium heat. Do not add oil.

Toast for about 3 minutes until fragrant and golden in color. Keep a close eye on it; raw coconut will burn quickly!

Spread some cream of coconut onto a plate and dip the rim of a rocks glass in it. Follow with a dip into the toasted coconut to rim your glass. Set aside.

In a cocktail shaker, add the rum, banana liqueur, lime juice, cream of coconut, and ice. Shake until extra cold.

Strain into your rimmed glass, garnish with the lime wedge, and enjoy.

FUN FACT: *Some people think The Toasted Coconut is an aphrodisiac. It's not, but maybe we don't tell them.*

AMARILLO

~ Texas, USA ~

Amarillo is a city replete with weathered cowboys and wayward romantics. An essential western stopover town for gigging musicians, it was made famous by George Strait's classic country tune of the same name. The traveling bug and an adventurous spirit seem like prerequisites for visiting this historic town. Perhaps this is what prompted the creation of the "cadillac ranch": a line of ten classic cars with their heads buried in the sand and lined up like dominos in the desert. This perfectly bizarre ode to disrepair fits strangely well amid the desolate and arid surroundings.

And when the blazing heat of a north Texas summer hits you like a freight train loaded with habanero hot sauce, there's nothing quite like a refreshing cocktail to give you some respite from the heat. So find some shade, kick back, and mix up this citrus and Tajin cocktail that'll make you feel like an outlaw in a lawless land.

The DESERT ROAD

In a land where desert desolation meets the perdurable American plains, The Desert Road delivers a vibrant citrus flavor with a kick of Tajin to spice up your stay in this historic western U.S. city. This cocktail delivers big flavor—after all, everything's bigger in Texas!

SERVES 1

Tajin seasoning to rim the glass (see Note)

1 grapefruit wedge

2 oz (60 ml) blanco tequila

¼ cup fresh grapefruit juice

splash of grapefruit soda

lime wedge, to garnish

Pour Tajin seasoning onto a small plate. Rub half the rim of a double rocks glass with the grapefruit wedge and dip the rim into the Tajin.

Fill your glass with ice. Add the tequila and grapefruit juice.

Top off with grapefruit soda and a squeeze of lime.

NOTE: *The original Tajin seasoning is based on a sauce recipe created in Zapopan, Jalisco, by a grandmother lovingly referred to as "Mama Necha." For a makeshift home recipe, blend together a desired amount of paprika, chili powder, dried lime zest, cumin, garlic powder, onion powder, coriander, cayenne, coarse sea salt, and sugar.*

MEDELLÍN

~ Colombia ~

If you haven't visited Colombia yet, I highly encourage you to make the trip. It's endlessly beautiful and populated with some of the kindest folks you'll ever meet. The northern city of Medellín is certainly no exception. Nestled amid picturesque deep-green hills and mountains, the city has a palpable vibrancy that really must be experienced firsthand.

Medellin, the capital of Antioquia province, is known as the "city of eternal spring" due to its comfortable climate and year-round warm weather. This idyllic climate does much for the fertility of the soil in the area, and everything from sorghum and rice, to bananas and orchids grow prolifically here. The city has become well-known for its ability to grow exotic fruits and vegetables year-round.

Colombia is also known for something that we all love. Ground into a powder, it's a sure-fire way to get that much-needed energy boost at your next party. Ingest even just a small amount, and you'll feel the effects almost immediately. The U.S. imported over 800 million kilos of it in 2020 alone.

We're of course talking about coffee.

You were thinking coffee, right?

Well ... now you are, so let's make an iced coffee chocolate cocktail and call it a night.

The DROGO DESPIERTO

When your eyelids grow heavy from the weight of the day, you need a Colombian concoction with a kick. Say *hola* to the Drogo Despierto—a chocolate and coffee cocktail that'll stimulate the spark and scintillate the senses.

SERVES 1

2 oz (60 ml) bourbon

1 oz (30 ml) cold brew coffee (preferably Colombian)

½ oz (15 ml) chocolate liqueur

½ oz (15 ml) cream

drizzle of dark chocolate syrup, to garnish

Add the bourbon, coffee, liqueur, cream, and ice to a shaker and shake what your mama gave you (while shaking the cocktail). Strain into a martini glass and decorate with a chocolate syrup drizzle. (Other great garnishes are a coffee bean, a sprinkle of nutmeg, or a fresh sprig of mint.)

FUN FACT: *Saint Drogo of Sebourg is the patron saint of coffee, and it's rumored that if you say his name three times in front of a mirror, your friends will think you're having a mental episode.*

THE KLONDIKE
~ Canada ~

The Klondike region in northwestern Canada is a place of great beauty, endless wilderness, and, of course, brutally cold winter weather. During The Klondike Gold Rush of 1896–1899, this remote area east of Alaska gained international fame when throngs of hopeful gold prospectors flooded the region in search of riches. Some of the lucky few found wealth beyond their wildest dreams, but many went home empty-handed … if they made it home at all. These lands have attracted adventurers and fortune seekers for generations, and there is still gold to be found.

But if panning for gold or trekking through deep mountain snow doesn't sound like your cup of tea, have no fear: this book is for adventures of the *mind*. We won't ask you to *actually* exert any physical effort. So in the spirit of pretending, imagine yourself huddled around a hearth as the relentless winter winds of the Yukon rattle through the boards of your prospector's shanty and freeze you to the bone. We're talking deathly cold here—quite dissimilar to the slight chill you might feel when your thermostat drops below 70 degrees (20 degrees Celsius). Far removed from the subtle nip in the air that hits you when you've left your favorite cardigan at home during your leisurely autumn stroll through the park.

Your cozy modern lifestyle wouldn't prepare you for the hardened days of the Yukon Gold Rush. Is this starting to feel like an attack on your character?

I digress.

The point is: If you are trying to toughen up, we feel it's our duty to suggest something with a little extra kick. Say hello to the Klondike Sled Dog.

The KLONDIKE SLED DOG

This lusty libation swaps out cola for the heartier flavor profile of root beer. Add in some espresso, light cream, and a healthy dose of vodka, and you've got yourself all the ingredients for a cozy night in listening to the wind and wolves howl outside.

SERVES 1

crushed ice

2 oz (60 ml) vodka

1 shot of espresso

2 oz (60 ml) light cream

splash of root beer

3 coffee beans, to garnish

Fill a cocktail shaker with the ice. Add the vodka, espresso, and cream. Shake until thoroughly blended. Pour into a frosty mug over additional ice and top with a generous splash of root beer. Garnish with coffee beans for an extra wake-up crunch.

Substitute the cream for any of your favorite non-dairy milks, or, for a sweeter treat, use chocolate milk.

You can mix it up with your favorite cola in place of root beer.

TEQUILA

~ Mexico ~

Just as Scotch must be produced in Scotland and Champagne in the region of France by the same name, in order for a spirit to be called "tequila" it must be produced in the Mexican state of Jalisco (with exceptions given to a few municipalities outside of Jalisco).

Tequila's roots can be dated back to the Aztecs, who used the sap of the agave plant to create a fermented drink known as pulque. The version of tequila that we know today was first commercially distilled by—you guessed it—the Cuervo family in 1758, in the town of Tequila in Jalisco. Today, the idyllic town of Tequila has a population of around 40,000 and—as the birthplace of the eponymous liquor—is a bucket-list destination for any self-respecting tequila connoisseur.

The history of tequila is as fascinating and hazy as many of the nights spent drinking this devilish delight. Treat her right, and she'll be your best friend, but treat her wrong, and you're in for a world of trouble. As playwright William Congreve once mused about a woman scorned, "hell hath no fury" like this infamous intoxicant.

Love it or hate it, tequila has earned quite a reputation over the years, and though the production of this spirit is strictly local, its enjoyment is profoundly global. So here's a drink to honor all those agave aficionados out there: Adiós Pantalones.

Adiós
PANTALONES

We've all surely had a crazy night or two drinking tequila. Something about this spirit makes you want to throw caution to the wind and put it all out there, so to speak. If your Spanish ain't so good, the *Adiós Pantalones* translates to "goodbye pants" ... you get the idea.

SERVES 1

2 oz (60 ml) blanco
    tequila

1 oz (30 ml) fresh lime
    juice

½ oz (15 ml) agave nectar

1 teaspoon orange
    marmalade

lime twist, to garnish

Mix everything but the lime twist with ice in a cocktail shaker. Shake, shake, shake. Strain into a chilled coupe glass. Garnish with the lime twist. Try to keep your pants on.

CAPE COD

~ *Massachusetts*, USA ~

Cape Cod refers to the peninsula in Massachusetts that extends prominently eastward into the Atlantic Ocean, jutting out like an outstretched and flexing arm. Which is an appropriate comparison because flexing is something Cape Cod can certainly do—the area is famous for its seafood delicacies, such as clams, oysters, lobster, and striped bass, and has been a go-to beach vacation destination for generations. In fact, the Pilgrims first made landfall in 1620 in what is now Provincetown—a town located at the very tip of the cape.

Since Cape Cod is surrounded by the ocean, it makes sense that the lifestyle here is focused heavily on water-based activities. Fishing and boating is a way of life here, so a thriving cocktail culture was basically preordained.

Cape Codders are well known for their ability to throw a few back. The ubiquitous Cape Codder—a cocktail consisting of vodka, cranberry, and lime—was invented here, after all. It takes a certain level of drunk devotion to lay claim to a cocktail of such renown. I guess all that lazing around in the sun necessitates a steady diet of jubilation juice. What's a day at the beach without a few adult beverages anyway?

The
GREAT WHITE

Just like the great white sharks that are now a common sight off the coast of Cape Cod, this tasty cocktail's got bite! The optional egg white addition also makes it (vaguely) white in color ... so, yeah—this cocktail's name is *perfectly* apt.

SERVES 1

*handful of fresh
   raspberries*

2 sage leaves

1 oz (30 ml) lemon juice

2 oz (60 ml) gin

½ oz (15 ml) simple syrup

egg white (optional)

In a cocktail shaker, muddle the raspberries (reserving one for garnish), sage, and lemon juice. Add your gin, simple syrup, and egg white (if using) and give a vigorous shake. Strain into a coupe glass. Garnish with a fresh raspberry.

> **NOTE:** *Consuming raw egg white may increase your risk of foodborne illness. For us, we like to live a little.*

ISLE OF SKYE
~ Scotland ~

The Isle of Skye is one of those magical places that feels almost otherworldly. With dramatic scenery, rugged coastlines, and ancient castles shrouded in fog, this island in northern Scotland has a truly mysterious quality. This fact has led many directors over the years to choose Skye as the perfect backdrop for their films and TV shows. It is also home to a couple of Scotch distilleries.

To mention Scotland in a cocktail book without also mentioning their greatest creation, Scotch, may actually be illegal. Scotch whiskey—or Scotch *whisky*, depending on where you reside in the world and your need to correct people's spelling like a nitpicking little turd—is one of the world's most esteemed spirits.

However you spell it, this bronzed beauty is truly a sight to behold. A favorite of intellectuals and degenerate sots alike, this lovely liquor always seems to break down barriers and connect people from all walks of life.

Musicians swear by it. Authors—particularly cocktail book authors—consider it to be as essential as pen and ink ... or computer and word processor, as the times now dictate.

Scotch basically co-wrote some of the best songs and works of literature in history, so who's to say Scotland doesn't have some kind of supernatural power?

The GINGERSNAP

Did you know that less than 2 percent of the world's population are redheads? In Scotland, however, that jumps to somewhere between 6 and 13 percent. This cocktail, the Gingersnap, is a slightly sweet libation with just a touch of complex spice—an homage to all of our redheaded friends out there!

SERVES 1

2 oz (60 ml) blended Scotch whiskey

1 oz (30 ml) amaretto

2 dashes of Angostura bitters

½ oz (15 ml) ginger liqueur

squeeze of lemon juice

candied ginger, to garnish (optional)

 Fill a double rocks glass with ice. Add the ingredients and give a good stir. Garnish with candied ginger for an extra special treat.

NOTE: *Blended Scotch should have a smooth taste, similar to bourbon, but with a spicy finish. As one would guess, it's made by blending two types of whiskey: barrel-aged malt whiskey and grain whiskey. It's the perfect choice for this cocktail. You can also try switching out the ginger liqueur for butterscotch for a slightly softer, sweeter taste.*

AMALFI COAST
~ Italy ~

The Amalfi Coast refers to the 30-mile (48-kilometer) stretch of land along the southern part of the Sorrentine Peninsula in the Salerno province of Italy. This coastal region is famed for its gorgeous scenery, rugged shorelines, vineyards, and quaint seaside villages. The warm and welcoming climate attracts starry-eyed honeymooners and fanny-pack-wearing septuagenarians alike—all searching for that once-in-a-lifetime experience. The region is also known for producing some of the most sought-after lemons in the world: the sfusato amalfitano and the limone di Sorrento. The sfusato amalfitano is the key ingredient in the production of Pallini Limoncello—a delightful liqueur that is just the cherry on top of the region's venerable cuisine.

So, with that being said—are you ready to take that long-dreamed-of trip to Italy? Are you putting in the necessary hours to learn Italian prior to your trip?

Doubtful.

Let's be honest, this book's core demographic is monolingual ... *at best*, or maybe that's just me.

Luckily, Italians are known for speaking with their hands, so if you don't actually *speak* Italian, it would be wise to work on your hand gestures instead. Simply adding "o's" to the ends of words won't get you far here, unfortunately.

Once you've got your gesticulations down, the Amalfi Coast is ready to welcome you with open arms. The utopian climes have everything you've been dreaming of. And speaking of dreams, Italy's cocktail, the Limoncello Spritz, is a gosh darn dreamy delight.

LIMONCELLO SPRITZ

The Limoncello Spritz is a sweet treat with just enough bubbly delight to lighten the mood. Sip with good company in the sunshine or in your bathtub with your cat, Lorenzo. Who are we to judge?

SERVES 1

1 oz (30 ml) limoncello
1 scoop of lemon sorbet
6 oz (175 ml) prosecco
*grated lemon zest,
   to garnish*
*berry of your choice,
   to garnish*

Pour your limoncello into a large wine glass. Place a beautifully rounded scoop of lemon sorbet on top. Fill with chilled prosecco. Serve with a garnish of grated lemon zest, a seasonal berry of your choice, and a dessert spoon.

NOTE: *For a creamier, more decadent treat, try lemon, strawberry, or blackberry gelato in place of the sorbet.*

NEW ORLEANS

~ Louisiana, USA ~

The port city of New Orleans on the southern tip of Louisiana is a place of rich history and diverse cultural influences. The proud melting pot of traditions here has led to a burgeoning food scene that is unlike anywhere else. Cajun and Creole cuisines add their own unique spice to life here, and festivals like Mardi Gras have, for better or worse, secured New Orleans's spot as a bona fide party town.

Imagine this scene, if you will: A trumpet blares from a dim back alley and grabs your attention. The commotion makes you forget for a moment the relentless heat that soaks your shirt in a searing sweat. It's far too late in the night for celebration. Besides, how could anyone be untroubled by this infernal humidity? You put aside your fantasies of air conditioning and decide to follow the sounds of carefree jubilation echoing down a narrow street.

You arrive to find a group of people dancing wildly to the sound of a zydeco band deep in the groove. The seemingly impromptu event is a party, and everyone in attendance is blissfully unconcerned about tomorrow's obligations—if they have any at all. This is New Orleans—a place to let your hair down and lose your inhibitions. If you're looking to fit in here, having fun is a prerequisite.

The
LOVE SPELL

As you wander streets alive with blues and romance, stop to sip on the mysteriously delicious Love Spell. This concoction is a twist on the classic sidecar cocktail, with an added touch of bliss from the bayou.

SERVES 1

sugar to rim the glass

2 oz (60 ml) dark rum

1 oz (30 ml) orange liqueur

1 oz (30 ml) freshly squeezed lemon juice

large orange peel swath, to garnish

Prepare a chilled coupe glass with a dip of sugar on the rim (for a bit of authenticity, use raw sugar). Fill a cocktail shaker with ice. Pour the rum, liqueur, and lemon juice into the shaker and silently chant your darkest desires while shaking (this should last 15 seconds, 30 if you're ambitious), then pour into your prepared glass. Garnish with a flamed orange swath (see below).

Flaming an orange peel: This allows the natural oils to drip into your cocktail. Slice a large swath of orange peel, about 3 inches (7.5 cm) long. Hold a lit match between the outer surface of the peel and the cocktail, and carefully squeeze the warmed citrus oils into your drink. (Note of warning: this should make a quick burst of flame.) Finish by rubbing the rim with the peel and dropping it into your drink.

SAFETY NOTE: *If you're not good with fire, or you've had a few warm-up drinks, please skip the pyrotechnics.*

MONTREAL

~ Canada ~

Montreal is the second most populous city in Canada, after Toronto. This French-speaking city along the Saint Lawrence River is Canada's epicenter for arts and culture and is known as a foodie town. With so much to do and see in "the city of festivals," it's hard to *not* have a good time.

But before traveling to Montreal, it should be asked: do you play—or have a fundamental knowledge of—hockey?

Yes? Please, enter.

No? Enter at your own risk.

Without a rudimentary understanding of the game of hockey—the players, rules, and history—you mark yourself as an obvious outsider. You may be able to survive the notoriously mean-spirited Canadians by name-dropping the prime minister or stating distances in kilometers, but if conversation goes more in depth and you accidentally say "ice hockey" instead of simply "hockey," the jig is up for you.

It's really not a lot to ask that you at least understand some basic principles of the Canadian national religion.

But if you *really* don't have the time to learn about hockey, due to the wonderfully informative nature of this book, you now *can* at least name drop "the city of festivals" in conversation or mention how you know Montreal to be the second biggest city in Canada. For anything beyond that, I recommend you belly up to the nearest bar, throw on a Montreal Canadiens hockey game, and learn a few things about *les habitants*. Or, you know, read something else.

The HAT TRICK

This Canadian comfort delivers a deliciously smoky flavor on ice. If you're new to hockey, or sports references in general, a hat trick occurs when a player scores three goals in a single game. The sugar, bourbon, and maple syrup combo in this cocktail is a three-pronged beast that's sure to score points with your friends.

SERVES 1

spoonful of pure maple syrup

pinch of fine granulated sugar

2 dashes of Angostura bitters

2 oz (60 ml) good-quality bourbon

orange wedge and swath, to garnish

cherry, to garnish

FOR SMOKING YOUR GLASS

food-safe cedar plank

brulee torch

First, smoke the glass (best done outside for safety). Light the center of the cedar plank on fire with the brulee torch, then invert your cocktail glass over the flame. The flame will extinguish and smoke will fill the glass. Let sit for a couple of minutes—take this time to have all your ingredients prepped before you turn the glass over so you can maximize the smoky goodness. And be sure the plank is contained in a fire-proof sink or bucket when you're done.

With all your ingredients prepped, turn over the smoke-filled glass. Quickly muddle the maple syrup, sugar, and bitters in the glass, then add ice and bourbon, and stir. Squeeze the orange wedge over your drink and garnish with the orange swath and cherry (we love Luxardo cherries for an extra decadent treat).

HOT TIP: *If you want to be really fancy, you can candy your orange swath ahead of time with maple syrup.*

SHANGHAI

~ China ~

Shanghai, on China's eastern coastline, is the country's most heavily populated city. This massive port is a hub of business, manufacturing, tourism, and culture and has earned the nickname of "the showpiece of China" due to its many diverse offerings. If you find yourself here, be sure to check out The Bund, a waterfront area where you can stroll along the boardwalk to sightsee, window-shop, people-watch, or just whistle dixie.

The word Shanghai means "on the sea" in Mandarin because ... well because it is *on the sea*, obviously. For whatever reason, coastal communities seem to always bring their own unique flavor to the spice of life. I guess sea air has a way of seasoning things in a way that makes life just a bit more colorful.

Maybe this goes back to the heyday of sailing, when sailors would arrive in port and share ideas and customs from all over the world. I can't say for certain. I mean I *could*, but that would require a level of research that I'm either not ready for or completely unwilling to undertake.

Here is a tidbit of research for you though: Shanghai is often called "the Paris of the east." And seeing as Paris is the city of love, we thought Shanghai's cocktail name should show some love. Say hello to the Coming Up Roses.

COMING UP ROSES

Nothing says "I love you" quite like roses—except maybe chocolate—but for this cocktail recipe, we're going with roses. This delightful libation is how we show our love to you, the reader. Rose syrup, rose water, and a few other choice ingredients; what's not to love?

SERVES 1

1 oz (30 ml) vanilla rose syrup

2 oz (60 ml) vodka

1 oz (30 ml) fresh lemon juice

1 oz (30 ml) ginger beer

edible flowers, to garnish (optional)

VANILLA ROSE SYRUP

2 cups rose water

2 cups white sugar

pinch of salt

1 tablespoon good-quality vanilla extract

First make the vanilla rose syrup. You can find rose water in the Asian section of many grocery stores. Combine the rose water, sugar, and salt in a small saucepan over a medium heat for about 5–7 minutes, stirring frequently until the sugar dissolves. Remove from the heat, add the vanilla, and let the aromas marry for a minute or two. If you'd like a rich pink hue, add a drop or two of red food coloring. Allow the syrup to cool. Any extra syrup will keep in a sealed container in the refrigerator for a few days.

To make the cocktail, add ice to a highball glass. Pour in your ingredients and give it a good stir. If you really want to woo your drinking-mate (or yourself), garnish with edible flowers.

VISBY

~ Sweden ~

The island of Gotland off Sweden's south-eastern coast is home to one of Scadinavia's best-preserved medieval cities: Visby. Known as "the city of roses and ruins", Visby is celebrated for its historical structures including a 2-mile-long defensive stone wall surrounding the city, as well as numerous church ruins, which led to the city being listed as a UNESCO World Heritage site in 1995. The name "Visby" actually comes from Old Norse and means "pagan place of sacrifice".

But don't let the flower-laden girls playing a vaguely sinister version of "Ring around the Rosie" in front of that large wood pyre fool you—Sweden is a place full of kind and friendly people. Those macabre Norse religious ceremonies are a thing of the past.

Mostly.

In addition—and perhaps more importantly—Sweden is known to have an abundance of beautiful people. That alone should be more than enough reason to take a trip in search of those fabled seductresses and seductress-men. (If you're wondering, yes: "seductress-men" IS the preferred term for men who exhibit a certain je ne sais quoi. I don't make the rules.)

And if *that* isn't reason enough (though it should be), Sweden also has an abundance of natural beauty to keep you endlessly enraptured.

The MAIDEN

Could you really make a cocktail inspired by Sweden *without* using aquavit? Probably ... but we couldn't resist the temptation. Hence, The Maiden: a refreshingly sweet elixir featuring that oh-so-delightful liquor made famous by those cheeky Scandinavians.

SERVES 1

1 tablespoon poppy seeds

1 tablespoon granulated sugar

1 lime wedge

3 fresh sweet strawberries

2 oz (60 ml) aquavit

¼ oz (10 ml) honey simple syrup

½ oz (15 ml) freshly squeezed lime juice

splash of ginger beer or soda water

HONEY SIMPLE SYRUP

1 cup honey

1 cup water

To make the simple syrup, combine the honey and water in a small saucepan. Bring to a gentle boil and simmer until the honey is completely dissolved, then chill. It can be stored in a sealed container and will easily last 2 weeks in the fridge.

In a small saucepan, heat the poppy seeds over a medium heat until they pop, about 1 minute. Remove from the heat and stir in the granulated sugar. Wet the rim of a coupe glass with the lime wedge and dip in the poppy seed sugar.

Sprinkle two of the strawberries with a pinch of sugar and muddle well. Slice the remaining strawberry and reserve for garnish. Fill a cocktail shaker with ice and add the aquavit, muddled strawberries, honey simple syrup, and lime juice. Shake and strain into the rimmed coupe glass, then garnish with the extra sliced strawberry. Top with ginger beer (or soda water).

NOTE: *Aquavit is made like gin, but with caraway instead of juniper. The first flavor impression is caraway and rye bread, with finishes of fennel, anise, and clove.*

MOSCOW

~ Russia ~

Moscow, the capital of Russia, is also the country's most populous city. Famed for its architecture, culture, and history, it is also famous for another thing: vodka. Over the years, Russia and vodka have become roughly synonymous, due in no small part to the tendency of its denizens to imbibe a substantial amount of this clear spirit. The Russians also have a solid claim to having invented it, as it is widely believed that around the year 1430, a monk named Isidore distilled the first recipe inside the Kremlin in Moscow. That's right, a monk is believed to have invented vodka. See, Mom, drinking is a godly pursuit!

FUN FACT: *Did you know that one time, the Russians took their partying so seriously that Moscow ran out of vodka? Can you imagine that? Of course you can—you bought this silly cocktail book, you cheeky boozehound.*

Many have said that vodka is the most versatile alcohol out there, and it's hard to argue against that. You can add vodka to basically anything if you need to kick things into gear.

Vodka cranberry? Obviously.

Vodka grapefruit? Too easy, mate.

Vodka Cheerios? Now we're getting somewhere.

But if you want to honor the true Russian tradition, drink it neat.

POCHEMUCHKA

The Russian word "pochemuchka" translates roughly to mean an overly curious child who asks too many questions. So if you find yourself dealing with that sort of nuisance, perhaps a coffee-based drink will help you perk up and get on their level. Worst-case scenario, you have a cocktail to sip on as you ignore the onslaught of questions being hurled in your direction.

SERVES 1

*6 oz (175 ml) strong
   brewed coffee or
   French press coffee*

*2 oz (60 ml) good vodka
   (or more to your taste)*

*1 oz (30 ml) crème de cacao
   (or chocolate syrup)*

¼ cup milk

*whipped cream,
   to garnish*

*drizzle of chocolate syrup,
   to garnish*

In an Irish coffee mug, add the coffee, then the vodka and crème de cacao. To steam the milk, if you don't have a fancy milk steamer, add it to a microwave-safe jar with a screw-top lid. Do not fill the jar more than halfway. Screw the lid on tightly, then vigorously shake for 30–60 seconds until the milk is foamy. Microwave without the lid for 30 seconds, but cover the jar with paper towel to avoid splashing, then immediately pour into your mug. Garnish with whipped cream and a drizzle of chocolate syrup.

QUITO

~ Ecuador ~

E cuador is a truly fascinating destination for any adventurer. With stunning national parks, the Galapagos Islands, hot springs, waterfalls, white-sand beaches, and rain forests, there is no shortage of things to do and see in this South American gem. Quito, the second-highest capital city in the world, is a destination unto itself. Featuring stunning colonial architecture, historic churches, and beautiful cathedrals, Quito (along with Krakow, Poland) was the first city in the world to be officially recognized as a UNESCO World Heritage Site in 1978. The city is also known as "the Florence of the Americas" due to its many colorful red-tile roofs, Spanish colonial architecture, and a layout reminiscent of European cities.

With so much to see and do in Ecuador, you don't need to work hard to spend all your money. So if you find you've exhausted your friends and family with your repeated pleas for "just a little traveling cash" while you're in Ecuador, look on the bright side: there are certainly worse places you could be. In fact, getting by on a shoestring budget is actually quite achievable in this equatorial country.

However, if you *are* on a shoestring budget, maybe keep your expectations in check. After all, fortune favors the gold, amigo.

But have no fear, there are plenty of budget-friendly activities in Quito to keep you occupied until some traveling cash comes through. You might even be able to make an extra buck or two mixing up cocktails using the recipes from this book. You're welcome.

PIÑA LOCO

As wanderlusts, we pride ourselves on drifting off the beaten path. But from time to time, one must relinquish oneself to a guilty tourist pleasure. In South America, guides love pushing this jazzy little drink to give the folks a giggle. The drifting can follow. Just find your way back to the buffet by dinner time.

SERVES 1

2 oz (60 ml) coconut rum

2 oz (60 ml) fresh pineapple juice

½ oz (15 ml) grenadine or cherry juice

freshly grated nutmeg, to garnish

slice of pineapple, to garnish

Pour all the ingredients except the garnishes over ice into a rocks glass and mix it up with your swizzle stick. Sprinkle with a bit of nutmeg, and garnish with a slice of fresh pineapple.

WROCLAW

~ Poland ~

Due to its large demographic of university students (over 130,000 of 'em), Wroclaw, Poland, is considered to be a very youth-oriented city. With such a large population of young'uns, Wroclaw naturally has an abundance of exciting events and entertainment to keep one amused, as well as a thriving food and drinking culture. Situated on the Oder River in western Poland, the city actually boasts one of the oldest restaurants in Europe: Piwnica Świdnicka, which opened its doors in 1273. Wroclaw also has an interesting fascination with guitar legend Jimi Hendrix and holds an annual festival in his honor. In 2019, the city set a Guinness World Record when 7423 people played the Hendrix hit "Hey Joe" in unison.

As a reader of this silly cocktail book, it's likely that you have at least *some* interest in alcohol and drinking culture. And that's good news—because this town is full of folks just like you, who want nothing more than a good time out of life.

Case in point: "The Festival of Good Beer" held every year there (not at the same time as the Hendrix festival, unfortunately).

What is this festival, you ask?

It's a FESTIVAL OF GOOD BEER ... like the name suggests. What more do you need to know?

So if you happen to find yourself in Wroclaw, you may as well surround yourself with like-minded people and bask in the joy of drinking beer—it's truly a cause worthy of celebration!

The STOUT and STORMY

For a city filled with university students and youth culture, we thought it might be a good idea to offer a tamer drink to offset all the partying. The Stout and Stormy is our solution: a beer-based libation with ginger syrup and a bit of lime juice. Slow things down a tad, will ya?

SERVES 1

¾ oz (25 ml) fresh-pressed
  lime juice

1 oz (30 ml) ginger syrup

12 oz (360 ml) milk stout
  or cream stout

lime wedge, to garnish

GINGER SYRUP
1 cup brown sugar
1 cup water
½ cup sliced fresh ginger

To make the ginger syrup, warm the brown sugar and water in a small saucepan over a medium heat and stir until the sugar dissolves. Add the sliced ginger and let steep over a low heat for about 10 minutes. Remove from the heat, cover, and allow to sit for an additional 30 minutes before straining into a container, discarding the ginger. The syrup will keep in a sealed container in the fridge for 5 days.

To make the cocktail, vigorously shake the lime juice and ginger syrup together and strain into a collins glass. Add the milk stout on top—float it if you can by pouring it gently over the back side of a spoon. Serve with a wedge of lime.

TOKYO

~ Japan ~

Tokyo, the capital city of Japan on the country's eastern coastline, is recognized as the world's largest urban economy and an international hub of business and finance, and the dining and entertainment options are nearly endless. Be sure to check out one of Tokyo's many excellent izakaya bars, where traditionally smaller and/or cheaper plates of food are served along with alcoholic beverages. These establishments are common after-work meeting places for Tokyoites, and also serve as jumping-off points for further eating and drinking.

Fueled up from an izakaya and in search of the perfect karaoke bar, you may find yourself faced with the scramble crossing at Shibuya subway station, which allows pedestrians to cross in all directions. It's the busiest pedestrian crossing in the world, sometimes with as many as 3000 people crossing at one time.

Which makes sense because Tokyo is the most populous city on earth. Did you know that? You did?

Well-lah-dee-dah, look at Mr./Ms. Smartypants! Don't act so high and mighty; anyone could Google that fact (as this author did). Did you also know that the Japanese have the second-longest life expectancy in the world (second only to people who live in Hong Kong)? You knew that too? Well, maybe *you* should be the one writing the damn book!

The reasons for Japan's high life expectancy are many, but surely all that sushi and saké play a significant role. For this reason, it seems prudent that you consume as much sushi and saké as you can to prolong your life.

Or maybe *you* have some better ideas??

The HONEY PLUM SOUR

Plums come with some badass symbolism in Japanese culture. Plums are one of the earliest crops to blossom in spring, and thus their blooms are a symbol of bounty, prosperity, and the start of the farming season. Plum trees, known as Ume trees, are also said to ward off evil spirits. For us, we'll mix them with good spirits for an extra ounce of good luck.

SERVES 1

2 oz (60 ml) Japanese Whiskey

2 dashes bitters of your choice

1 oz (30 ml) honey plum sauce

1 oz (30 ml) fresh lemon juice

splash of soda water

thin wedge of plum or sliced lemon, to garnish

HONEY PLUM SAUCE
6 very ripe red plums, chopped

2 cups water

1½ cups honey

To make the honey plum sauce, simmer the ingredients gently for about half an hour, until the plums are broken down. Strain and discard any remaining solids. The sauce will keep refrigerated in an airtight container for 2 weeks. To make the cocktail, combine all the ingredients, except the soda water, in a highball glass over ice. Stir. Top with soda water. Garnish with a thin wedge of fresh plum or a slice of lemon.

96

GALWAY

~ Ireland ~

The port city of Galway on Ireland's west coast is the midpoint of The Wild Atlantic Way, a popular tourist trail stretching some 1500 miles (2400 kilometers) along the Atlantic coast. Like much of Ireland, Galway has a mild oceanic climate, but ask any of the roughly 80,000 Galway residents and they would describe their city as anything *but* mild. The bohemian vibe and uninhibited culture of the city make this a very appealing destination for travelers looking to have a bit of fun.

With Ireland giving so much to the world over the course of its history— from scientific advances like splitting the atom, color photography, and the submarine to influential works of literature and music—it's almost ironic that the Irish have become so renowned for their drinking culture ... though it is a point of pride for many.

And here's some good news: if you're an English speaker, you'll be able to take in Ireland's famous drinking culture, speak your native tongue, *and* be able to understand about 80 percent of the roughly-coherent words spoken to you by the friendly folks of Ireland. But mix in a bit of drinking, and that rate of coherence can drop significantly.

So in order to help you out a bit, if a local asks you, "What's the craic?," this common expression can be thought of as similar to "How are you?" To answer that question like a local, you might respond with "Divil a bit," which is roughly akin to saying "Not much." But if the drinking picks up considerably (as it's likely to), you're on your own, friend.

Hot
APPLE TODDY

If you're heading to Ireland, why not mix up an Irish whiskey drink? This little delight will get you feeling right in an instant: honey to soothe your throat, hot apple cider to warm your soul, and a healthy dose of whiskey to dull your senses. What could be better?

SERVES I

1 teaspoon honey

2 oz (30 ml) whiskey

4 oz (125 ml) hot apple cider

1 teaspoon butter

lemon wedge, to garnish

cinnamon stick, to garnish

Drizzle the honey into the bottom of a mug, then add your whiskey and give it a little stir. Top with the hot apple cider and butter. Garnish with a lemon wedge and cinnamon stick. (For an extra cozy treat, try placing a big slice of baked apple in the bottom of your mug before building the cocktail.)

CAIRO

~ Egypt ~

There is little that can be said about Cairo, Egypt, that isn't basically common knowledge. Attractions like the pyramids, the Sphinx, and the Sahara Desert have had a powerful, almost mystical, pull on people the world over for centuries. But that's all ancient history.

The Cairo of today is worlds different than it was in the days of the pharaohs. The city was a focal point for the Arab Spring movement—the 2011 Egyptian revolution that led to the ouster of then-president Hosni Mubarak. Despite its storied and expansive history, Cairo is a city still searching for the best version of itself. But its mystique is still alive and well and you can go searching for them in the city's souks and bazaars. Even a landmark like the Nile River has a magical draw.

If the Nile proves too enticing to ignore, consider taking a felucca boat tour to get a glimpse of Cairo and the surrounding area from the water. A felucca is a traditional wooden sailboat used primarily in the eastern Mediterranean. A relaxing ride down the Nile may be just what you need to unwind from a busy day walking the streets and shopping the many bazaars of Cairo. Drifting aimlessly is what you do best anyway, am I right?

The DESERT KISS

The featured ingredient in The Desert Kiss cocktail is a shrub. A shrub is a nonalcoholic syrup primarily consisting of fruit, sugar, and vinegar. Shrubs are often consumed in hot, dry climates to refresh and reinvigorate the salivary glands. The flavor profile is not for everyone (this author included), but the sweet and acidic taste (allegedly) unlocks some unique flavors to tickle the senses. For a nonalcoholic option, take out the vodka and drink your shrub straight.

SERVES 1

1 oz (30 ml) homemade shrub

2 oz (60 ml) vodka

4 oz (125 ml) soda water (or tonic for more sweetness)

sprig of basil, mint, or rosemary, to garnish

SHRUB

1 cup sugar of your choice

1 cup apple cider vinegar

fresh fruit of your choice

To make the shrub, heat the sugar and vinegar in a saucepan, stirring constantly, until the sugar is dissolved. Add the fruit and simmer for 5 minutes to release the juices. Remove from the heat, cool, and strain through a cheesecloth (muslin) into a storage jar. Let rest in the refrigerator for 2 days prior to mixing into your cocktail. (And if you're in a rush, lots of craft cocktail stores sell premade shrubs!)

For the cocktail, pour the shrub and vodka over ice into a collins glass, top with soda water, and give it a light stir. Garnish with complementary herbs like basil, mint, or rosemary.

NOTE: *With homemade shrubs, you can get really creative with the flavor combinations. For your fruits, ripe berries are great, but you can use apples, figs, plums, or even rhubarb. For sugars, experiment with white, raw, and brown for different flavor depths. For vinegar, apple cider is reliable, but you can try varieties of white or balsamic as well.*

CAPE TOWN
~ South Africa ~

The city of Cape Town on the west coast of South Africa is an excellent jumping-off point for all sorts of adventures. Take a cable car ride up to the top of Table Mountain, go on safari, zip-line, or surf one of the many stellar breaks nearby. Also be sure to check out the Cape of Good Hope—an important beacon for sailors making their way around Africa through waters infamous for unpredictable and inclement weather.

Remember that scene from *The Endless Summer* when Mike and Robert look like they are having a blast on some amazing waves off the coast of Cape Town? That could be you. But in the likely event that you don't actually surf, we recommend heading east to the nearby town of Stellenbosch for a bit of wine-tasting. Stellenbosch has an ideal climate for growing grapes—the cabernet sauvignon produced here is widely acclaimed. Take your time and explore all the vineyards in the area for a perfectly relaxing, low-stress daytime activity.

But if all the touring and wine-tasting doesn't do the trick, make yourself a Soulmate and just sit there like a bump on a log.

The SOULMATE

Brandy and cola is well-known as the most popular cocktail in South Africa. South Africans have been distilling brandy since 1672, so they've had a long time to perfect their craft. It took 214 more years for Coca-Cola to be invented (in Atlanta, Georgia). Fast forward nearly 50 more years to the 1930s, when the two found one another in this now iconic Cape Town cocktail. We believe soulmates are worth the wait. One sip, and you're lost in fizzy bliss. This cocktail will simultaneously cool you down and perk you up for your next adventure.

SERVES 1

2 oz (60 ml) South African brandy
6 oz (185 ml) ice-cold cola
¼ oz (10 ml) lemon juice
cherries, to garnish

Assemble with ice in a highball glass and garnish with a lemon twist. You can substitute lime or orange for the juice and garnish to mix things up!

BYRON BAY

~ Australia ~

Byron Bay is a small beach town of about 10,000 people on the east coast of Australia, in the state of New South Wales. This perfectly picturesque oceanside community is famous for its laid-back vibe and friendly atmosphere, with all the surf, sun, and sand you could want—and surprisingly raucous nightlife to boot. The town's many restaurants and pubs often showcase local musicians from the thriving music scene, while the yearly Byron Bay Bluesfest attracts big-name acts from all over the world. After you've had your fill of the music and nightlife in Byron Bay, the nearby beaches are great for surfing or just catching a tan.

Oh, and did you know that a few big-name celebrities are now calling Byron Bay home? Chris Hemsworth frequents the area, and although he is happily married (sad face), maybe there's a cute Aussie bloke in his entourage that you could entice into taking a late-night dip in the Pacific with you. Even though you're unlikely to snag Thor himself, you'll at least be able to tell your friends about this one time when you walked past (and shamelessly selfied in front of his house).

So go ahead and throw on your favorite pair of sunnies and stroll along Jonson Street to get a taste of the laid-back yet fun-loving Byron Bay lifestyle. However, if relaxing or having fun aren't your cup of tea, might I suggest putting this book down and checking out *Debby Downer's Guide to Traveling*? It might have a better grasp on what you're looking for.

It's no worries here, mate. Byron Bay is sure to please.

FIRST BASE
on the BEACH

This little concoction is a spin on the ubiquitous "sex on the beach" cocktail. With the addition of jello, the "first base on the beach" always goes down easy. Sure, it may be less worthy of bragging to your friends about, but it still packs a punch. Plus, it's likely to result in fewer spills (and sand in unsavory places).

MAKES 12 SHOTS
(2 OZ/60 ML EACH)

1½ cup pineapple juice

6 oz (175 g) packet peach or cranberry gelatin

1 cup vodka

1 cup lemon-lime soda

In a medium saucepan, bring the pineapple juice to a boil, then dissolve the gelatin packet into the juice. Add your booze and soda and stir well. Pour into small vessels and chill in the refrigerator for about 2.5 hours before serving.

GOBI DESERT
~ Mongolia ~

The Gobi Desert is the sixth-largest desert in the world, covering a vast expanse of land that stretches from northern China to southern Mongolia. The Gobi is a rain shadow desert, where the Tibetan Plateau to the southwest blocks off moisture and causes only minimal precipitation to fall. Despite its arid climate, the Gobi Desert is still home to a diverse array of plants and animals that have adapted to the difficult environment. But in terms of global travel, it's about as remote as you can get.

So if you're looking for the end of the earth, someplace no one will track you down—or probably even bother looking for you—then Mongolia's Gobi Desert is as good a place as any to head to.

Though it begs the question: What are you running from? Why the sudden need to disappear? You're sending up some red flags here, friendo.

Maybe you're working on becoming a more interesting and well-traveled human. Or maybe that superlative you were awarded in high school ("most likely to do the least with their life") has finally spurred you to action ... If only they could see you now!

Whatever the case may be, if you find yourself in this remote corner of the world, go ahead and mix up a Snow Leopard and disappear into your peaceful oblivion.

The
SNOW LEOPARD

GOBI DESERT, MONGOLIA

Mongolia is home to the rare and endangered snow leopard. This big cat is usually solitary and very elusive. Much like the writer of this book. We can't promise you'll see a snow leopard on your adventures, but perhaps have a few cocktails and donate some dollars to animal conservation. The wild things will thank you.

SERVES 1

sugar to rim the glass

1 oz (30 ml) black currant liqueur

½ oz (15 ml) vanilla syrup

2 oz (60 ml) vodka

1 oz (30 ml) whole milk

sprig of rosemary, to garnish (optional)

Moisten and dip half the rim of a stemless glass in sugar. In the glass, combine the black currant liqueur and vanilla syrup and give it a light swizzle. Fill the glass with ice. Next, fill a cocktail shaker with ice, and add the vodka and milk. Shake vigorously for a full minute. Pour delicately into your cocktail glass. Garnish with a sprig of rosemary.

BELÉM

~ Brazil ~

Belém is the capital and largest city in the state of Pará in northern Brazil. Despite being lesser known than cities like Rio de Janeiro and São Paulo, Belém has a vibrant and friendly culture among its 2 million residents. And with a tropical rain forest climate, this metropolis of the Brazilian Amazon brings the kind of sultry heat Brazil is known for.

And if it's your aim to surround yourself with beautiful scenery—or beautiful people—there really is no place better than Brazil. This huge country in South America consistently ranks among the top places in the world to see beautiful people—often coming in at the oh-so-sweet spot of #1.

Maybe it's something in the waters of the Amazon that can explain Brazil's prolific production of beautiful people.

Whatever the cause, Brazil is doing more than its part to counteract the plethora of uggos being produced in other parts of the world (not you, you're gorgeous). So do yourself a favor and hit the gym before your next Brazilian vacation ... you'll be glad you did!

The SUNNY SIDE

BELÉM, BRAZIL

Brazil's national spirit is cachaça, which is a hard liquor made of sugarcane. Cachaça has a rich history dating back to the 1500s, when it was invented by enslaved people working in sugarcane mills. Cachaça's exports are limited, and the majority of the product stays in Brazil, so we suggest substituting rum in this cocktail.

SERVES 1

3–4 chunks of fresh pineapple (or exotic fruit of your choice)

1 teaspoon cane sugar

1 oz (30 ml) cachaça or light rum

splash of soda water

lime wedge, to garnish

In a rocks glass, place your fruit and sugar. Muddle well into a nice pulp. Top with your spirit, a splash of soda water, and give it a stir. Garnish with any remaining pineapple and a wedge of lime.

NOTE: *While you can substitute rum for the cachaça because it's far more accessible, it's quite a different spirit. Rum is usually made from fermenting and then distilling sugarcane by-products like molasses—which gives it a sweet, toasted taste. Cachaça is made directly from sugarcane itself, which gives it more of an earthy, grassy flavor profile.*

BARCELONA
~ Catalonia, SPAIN ~

If you don't want to look like a dang fool—or you don't want to look like *more* of a fool—this northeastern Spanish city is pronounced Barth-a-lona by locals (a "th" sound instead of an "s" sound).

Now that we've gotten that little clarification out of the way, let's move on to the more important things, like Spain's famous food, culture, and ... siestas.

Spaniards are famous for taking naps (siestas) in the afternoon each day.

Naps? In the afternoon?!

That's right, you'll be able to catch up on your Z's right in the middle of the day ... and nobody will bat an eye! (Because they'll also be sleeping.)

Siestas are an integral part of Spanish culture—perhaps the key component that allows one to go from watching a daytime FC Barcelona football match to gorging on evening tapas to staying out all night partying. You think you can achieve all of this on a mere seven hours of rest? Get real, amigo.

For all the slothful souls and slackers out there, midday naps are surely a welcome addition to the daily schedule. And for the go-get-em types, guess what? Siestas are widely believed to lower stress, increase energy, and improve both creativity and productivity. Maybe tell that to your boss the next time they catch you snoozing.

And when you stir from your slumber, grab some paella and a big ol' pitcher of *Siesta Para Seis*, a sangria concoction worthy of Barcelonian admiration.

You deserve it, amigo.

SIESTA PARA SEIS

The *Siesta Para Seis* is a pitcher of sangria for six, or—if you're feeling adventurous—a pitcher for one. If you plan to share with your friends, this drink is a great post-siesta pick-me-up. If you plan to drink this by yourself, it's a sleeping aid.

SERVES 6

3 cups seasonal fruit
¼ cup granulated sugar
½ cup Spanish brandy
25½ oz (750 ml) dry white Spanish wine (verdejo or sauvignon blanc)
6 oz (185 ml) soda water

Choose fresh, seasonal fruit. Peaches, apples, white grapes, and strawberries are great choices. Any fruit will do, as long as it's seasonal and delicious.

Chop or slice all the fruit, including the grapes, place in a large bowl and sprinkle with the sugar and brandy and gently stir. Allow to macerate overnight in the fridge, or as long as you can wait.

Place the fruit in a pitcher and add your dry white wine. Give it a nice stir.

To serve, pour into a wine glass with ice. Be sure to get a lovely assortment of fruit into each glass, and leave room to top it off with an ounce (30 ml) or so of soda water.

SANTO DOMINGO
~ Dominican Republic ~

The Dominican Republic is one of my favorite destinations in the Caribbean for a myriad of reasons that are as diverse as the country itself. There is maybe some debate on whether you should vacation in Santo Domingo or Punta Cana when you visit. Honestly, the country isn't huge and you can do both, but if you have to pick one, give Santo Domingo, the capital city, a try. It follows the rule of: when you have the choice, choose culture over all-inclusive. Santo Domingo is a wonderful cross-section of all the DR has to offer. It is one of the oldest cities in the Caribbean, with a cityscape that blends past and present with plenty of beautiful stops within a close drive. Take a trip to Parque Colon, where you can sip some cafe tinto while sitting in a square that dates back to the 16th century. Once you've soaked up enough history, grab your bathing suit and lounge on the white sands at either Juan Dolio or Guayacanes beaches.

Are you suffering from poor circulation, congestion, or the flu? Maybe your vitality needs rejuvenation? Well, the DR has what you need. It's called Mamajuana and it will take care of anything that ails you. It's part rum, part red wine, and part herbs and spices. Will it actually help fix your kidneys? I don't know, I'm not a doctor. I can, however, guarantee it will help you loosen up enough to show off all of those merengue skills you've been secretly practicing.

The best part is you can recover from your hangover on one of their many beautiful beaches. Is the sun too bright? Fine, take a trek in the lush jungles. The DR has something for everyone.

Mama's
MEDICINE

Mamajuana is a Dominican beverage said to give you an increase in vitality and energy—so sip responsibly, or with opportune timing. As legend has it, this sweet and fiery concoction claims to cure ailments and woes. We can't vouch for that ... but at the very least, it may help you seize the day. Buy a fun hat. Pet a pigeon. Call your mother. Whatever gets you feeling fine, while staying on the right side of the law.

SERVES 12

2 cups Dominican dark
*   rum*

8 cloves

6 allspice berries

4 star anise

2 cinnamon sticks

1 cup red wine

1 cup honey

In a sealable container, mix your rum and spices. Let steep in the refrigerator for a week. Once THAT long wait is done, add your wine and honey. Let steep at least one more day. It's like Mom always said: good things take time and patience is a virtue. Serve chilled in a shot glass.

GEIRANGER

~ Norway ~

Geiranger, in western Norway, is another destination that has earned a spot on the UNESCO World Heritage list. This small village of only about 200 people has a large appeal for international travelers and adventurers alike. With sweeping views of snow-covered peaks and huge waterfalls that cascade into the fjord below, Geiranger looks like an otherworldly dreamscape. Even though getting to this remote destination may be slightly less *AFJORDABLE* (relax ... I'm not proud of it either) than you had hoped, the town is worth every penny, and attractions like the Seven Sisters waterfall simply cannot be missed.

So there you have it—the reasons to visit Geiranger are numerous. But maybe you're coming here to connect to your Nordic roots, or maybe your Viking ancestors beckon you here from Valhalla. Or perhaps you're coming to get in touch with you inner Viking and pillaging and plundering ways.

Sure, you've never *actually* sacked or looted a village, but you *have* been burning bridges your whole life—maybe you have some Viking in you after all!

Whether your audacious behavior can be attributed to your actual genealogical roots can't be said for certain, but a visit to this land up north *may* help you feel more at peace with all your recklessness.

So in the spirit of recklessness, here's the Isbjørn to tempt those temerarious types.

The ISBJØRN

In Norway the name for polar bear is isbjørn ("ice bear"), but you'll need to head about 1100 miles (1800 km) north of Geiranger to the archipelago of Svalbard for your best chance to spot a real one. While this cocktail may not be quite as majestic as the beast it's named for, it will for sure keep you feeling warm and fuzzy on a snowy winter's eve. Kick start your Norwegian adventure with a healthy dose of Norway's prized spirit: aquavit.

SERVES 1

1 oz (30 ml) aquavit

½ oz (15 ml) honey

2 dashes bitters

crushed ice

3 oz (90 ml) chilled prosecco

lemon twist or star anise, to garnish

Combine the aquavit, honey, and bitters in a shaker. Add the crushed ice and shake extremely well to blend that honey. Strain into a chilled coupe glass, top with chilled prosecco, and garnish with your lemon twist. Star anise also makes an awesome-looking garnish.

NOTE: *Aquavit is made like gin, but with caraway instead of juniper. The first flavor impression is caraway and rye bread, with finishes of fennel, anise, and clove.*

CLARKE QUAY

~ Singapore ~

Singapore is too often skipped over as a travel destination for its nearby neighbors in southeast Asia. In part that is due to how easy it is to miss, tucked into the South China Sea; you'd need to squint at the map to realize you weren't looking at the southern tip of Malaysia. (Or maybe that's just me—I probably do need new glasses.) The other part is that people think it is much more expensive than a lot of other destinations in the region. The reality is the most expensive part about traveling throughout southeast Asia is the plane ticket to get there. Once there, skipping Singapore would be a mistake. It has a unique blend of colonial and modern architecture that you won't find in other countries, a thriving nightlife, and it is very clean.

Clarke Quay exemplifies these qualities well. While it is predominantly known for its thriving nightlife, that doesn't mean you should sleep in until the sun sets. Stroll through Fort Canning Park for beautiful gardens, scenic views, and to learn a bit about the area's history. Hop on a boat and take a tour along the Singapore River, and be sure to bring your camera.

Then, after you've played tourist for the better part of your day, put your parents to bed and get ready to party. The nearby Raffles Hotel actually invented the world-famous Singapore Sling cocktail, so you know the Singaporeans know a thing or two about having a good time. Plus, you can get a little taste of history to mix in with all your partying.

The MONARCH

This drink is crafted after the noteworthy Singapore Sling—the vibrantly pink go-to cocktail for ladies at the start of the 20th century. The birthplace of this drink, The Raffles Hotel Singapore, originally created the cocktail as a stealthy way for women to imbibe in public. Today, this hotel still slings their famous cocktail in wild numbers. Seekers of the boozy delight line up out the door for a taste ... so while you're sipping, buy one for the gal pal next to you!

SERVES 1

1 oz (30 ml) gin

1 oz (30 ml) sake

1 oz (30 ml) lime juice

½ oz (15 ml) maraschino cherry juice

2 oz (60 ml) lemon-lime soda

cherry and orange slice, to garnish

Add everything but the soda and garnishes to a cocktail shaker with ice and shake until well chilled. Strain into a highball glass filled with ice. Top with lemon-lime soda, and garnish with cherry and an orange slice.

SIARGAO ISLAND
~ The Philippines ~

Siargao is an island of about 170 square miles (440 square kilometers) on the eastern side of the Phillipine archipelago. Siargao played a large role in popularizing surfing in The Philippines, and has recently become known as "the surfing capital of The Philippines." With epic surf breaks like Cloud 9, it's no wonder that the area has become a bucket-list surf destination for many. But if surfing isn't your cup of tea, Siargao also has an abundance of white-sand beaches for lounging in the sun, coral reefs for snorkeling, and, for the more adventurous types, rock climbing and spelunking.

> **FUN FACT:** *Now let's talk about the elephant in the room. We give a lot of credit to Magellan for being the first person to circumnavigate the world, but that's a bunch of hogwash. The guy was killed by a poison arrow while trying to help take over a local village in what is now the Philippines three-quarters of the way through his journey. I mean props for not being a flat-earther, but c'mon.*

If you were to visit the Philippines, you may also never leave, but that would be by choice. The place has over 7000 islands to choose from. That's probably too many to visit in one trip, so for those who want a little bit of everything without breaking the bank, Siargao Island is an excellent option.

The GINPOM

The Philippines is one of the world's greatest consumers of gin. Right behind your great aunt Ethel. The GinPom is a quintessential easy Pinoy cocktail, using powdered pomelo drink mix for a tangy and sweet taste. Here we substitute fresh grapefruit or pomelo juice for convenience, but if you can find the powdered pomelo drink mix, you're a winner!

SERVES 1

2 oz (60 ml) dry gin

4 oz (125 ml) fresh grapefruit or pomelo juice

2 sprigs of basil

splash of grapefruit soda

grapefruit or pomelo slice, to garnish

Add the gin, grapefruit juice, and basil to a shaker and give it a good shake down. Strain into a coupe glass and top with a splash of grapefruit soda. Garnish with a slice of grapefruit or pomelo.

NOTE: Pomelos come in many varieties, and a good one should taste sweeter than a grapefruit. Slightly larger than a grapefruit, your pomelo should have chartreuse skin and light pink flesh.

PRO TIP: *For aromatic herbs in cocktails, it's important to spank them. Yes, you read that right. Lightly smacking the basil in your hands prior to adding it to your drink releases its aromas without crushing or bruising the tender leaves.*

PORTLAND

~ Maine, USA ~

So now, like so many Speedo-clad grandfathers before us, we head to the beach. The warm, tropical, and always sunny beaches of ... Portland, Maine? It's an essential stop on any bracing New England adventure. Famed for its scenic and rocky coastline, quaint lighthouses, and seafood, this Casco Bay port city is a must-see.

It's not exactly tropical, but at least there is an ocean to stare at while you sip THE classic cocktail of Maine: The Lobster Bisque Tequila Slammer.

Just kidding, that sounds gross.

But, because Maine is known for its lobster, we felt obligated to offer a drink with that signature red color. Even though it's not exactly a cocktail, there's nothing better than a red beer when the sun sinks low and you're staring out at the endless blue of the Atlantic.

FUN FACT: *A red beer is just as delicious when the sun rises. Red beer is an essential addition to any beer lover's repertoire, and it pairs really well with foggy Maine mornings and hangovers.*

Though the Clamato juice mixer may turn some people off, turning people off is kinda right in my wheelhouse. (If you're unfamiliar with Clamato juice, its two main ingredients are right there in the name ... clam and tomato, together at last.) Just give it a shot, and I promise you'll love it. I was once an ignorant non-believer too, but then my eyes were opened to a whole new world.

The PICKLED LOBSTER

Make your own spicy boozy pickles to enjoy in cocktails or right from the jar! After a rowdy night, a little hair of the dog always sets you right—and The Pickled Lobster will get you running on all cylinders in no time. And if you prefer *not* running on all cylinders, it can get you there just as easily.

SERVES 1

12 oz (360 ml) lager beer

3 oz (90 ml) Clamato juice

1 oz (30 ml) juice from the spicy cocktail pickles

SPICY COCKTAIL PICKLES

1 large lemon

3 small cucumbers, quartered lengthwise

1 garlic clove, sliced

⅓ cup Clamato juice

1/3 cup distilled white vinegar

2 teaspoons horseradish

½ teaspoon black peppercorns

½ teaspoon salt

1 dash hot sauce (to taste)

¼ cup vodka

To make the pickles, slice half the lemon into rounds. Pack the cucumbers, lemon rounds, and garlic into a 1 pint (473 ml) glass jar with a lid. In a small saucepan over a medium heat, combine the Clamato juice, juice from the other half of the lemon, white vinegar, horseradish, peppercorns, salt, and hot sauce. Bring to a boil, stirring occasionally. Remove from the heat and stir in the vodka. Pour the Clamato juice mixture over the cucumbers. Wipe the rim of the jar clean and seal with a lid. Allow to cool completely, then refrigerate until cold. The longer they sit, the better they taste. They'll keep in the refrigerator for up to 3 weeks.

To make the red beer, combine the ingredients in a pint glass and stir. Garnish with whatever your heart desires. Bacon, a donut, beef jerky, celery ... or a whole lobster claw.

NOTE: If you can't find Clamato juice, you can substitute it for tomato juice

145

BERLIN

~ Germany ~

The northeast German city of Berlin is another destination in this book that belongs to the "capital and largest city" category. We like to feature the largest city in each country for a myriad of reasons, not the least of which is simple mathematics (read: larger potential readership = larger potential earnings). But we're not *just* about that money money—we care about *all* of the aspects that make a destination unique. The unique points of interest in Berlin are numerous, but it's certainly worth mentioning the city's thriving art and museum scene. Street art, in particular, has become one of the city's calling cards, tracing its roots back to the days of the Berlin Wall, when artists would create murals and graffiti art as a form of self-expression. Due to its rapid proliferation—costing the city roughly €35 million a year to clean up— graffiti art is now illegal here unless it is expressly allowed by building owners. But there is still plenty of legal art to see—consider taking a walking tour of the city's street art, or head to Museum Island in the city's historic center, where you have five museums in close proximity so you can get more than your fill of history and culture.

Another lesser-known feature of Berlin is its waterways. Berlin has over 100 miles (160 kilometers) of navigable waterways, which is a lot. It's a bit like Venice in a way ... plus it's not sinking. Then, once you're back on land, you can start drinking. This is a cocktail book, so I'm not legally allowed to tell you to try Berlin's official beer, the Berliner Weisse, but between friends, you should. You should also try this cocktail creation in honor of Berlin, the Essen und Trinken.

ESSEN und TRINKEN

We would be remiss not to acknowledge BEER and GERMANY in a drinking book. Berliner Weisse is a light, tart beer often served with raspberry syrup. "Essen und Trinken" means eat and drink, and THAT is something we can all agree on.

SERVES 1

1 oz (30 ml) raspberry liqueur

6 oz (185 ml) hefeweizen or stout (or Berliner Weisse)

Pour your raspberry liqueur into a goblet. Top with a pour of your favorite German beer. We suggest hefeweizen, but it's also deliciously decadent with a chocolatey stout.

NOTE: *While you're stocked up on German beer, treat yourself to learning a good cheese dip recipe. Don't forget an ample supply of warm pretzels ... and bratwurst ... and schnitzel ... is anyone else feeling hungry?*

KOLKATA

~ India ~

If you don't recognize the name "Kolkata," that's likely because this huge east Indian city of roughly 15 million people was formerly known as "Calcutta." The name changed in 2001 to match the Bengali pronunciation. This bustling city may prove exasperating for anyone unaccustomed to navigating cities with such a high population density, but if you can handle all the hustle and bustle, then you will be rewarded with a truly unique and exceptional travel experience.

Did you know that India holds a world record for the country with the largest number of official languages?

What records do *you* hold?

Most egregious waste of space? *Least* valuable player?

Just kidding, I'm sure you're great. Maybe it'd be best to stop antagonizing the readers. After all, it's *you* who makes this all possible ... whatever *this* is.

Back to India: Have you tried their food? It's out of this world! Traditional Kolkata dishes like kosha mangsho (mutton curry) and macher jhol (fish curry) are sure to make your mouth water. The city is also famous for its street food, so you can grab a quick bite without losing too much time to a sit-down meal.

And if you're noshing on some delicious Indian cuisine, maybe consider a signature Indian cocktail to wash it all down? (This *is* a cocktail book, after all.)

Say hello to The Lucky Lassi.

The LUCKY LASSI

How would you like to taste the oldest smoothie ever invented? And no, we don't mean the mystery one lingering in the back of your fridge. Lassi is a blended yogurt drink with ancient roots dating back to 1000 BC in the region of Punjab in India. Considered a treat, the lassi was crafted to be cool and refreshing on hot summer days. This boozy version is a modern twist.

SERVES 2

2 cups Greek yogurt

2 cups fresh mango
   chunks

4 oz (125 ml) dark rum

1 cup coconut milk

½ teaspoon cardamom
   powder, plus extra
   to garnish

¼ cup clover honey

crushed ice

Add all the ingredients to a blender and blend until smooth. Pour into highball glasses with a wide straw. Garnish with a sprinkle of cardamom and drizzle in extra honey for more sweetness.

NOTE: *If you want an authentic Indian spirit, seek out Old Monk Rum, a dark Indian rum with strong vanilla notes dating back to the early 1950s. The rum was named after a beloved British monk in India who loved sampling locally distilled rums in the making.*

PARIS

~ France ~

What can be said of Paris that hasn't been said better by others many times before? Mentioning iconic landmarks like the Louvre, the Champs-Élysées, Notre Dame, and the Eiffel Tower feels a bit obvious, if not entirely redundant (but I've gone and done it anyway).

Cuisine? Umm, yeah you could say Paris knows a thing or two about that.

Music? Psssh, the city is teeming with musicians of the highest caliber, and it also attracts huge international acts like moths to a flame.

What about history? Oh sure, *maybe* somewhere in the city's 2000-year history you can find something to pique your interest.

Art? This is a city that inspired people like Victor Hugo, Ernest Hemingway, Edgar Degas, Gertrude Stein, Pablo Picasso, and James Joyce—a veritable who's who of the greatest writers and artists of all time. It's safe to say that Paris has more than enough art and culture to keep you occupied.

So what new information can I offer, you ask?

Very little.

My best advice would be to go experience the city yourself and stop listening to the ramblings of a whiskey-loving hack.

But if you *really* need something from me, maybe try this Paris-inspired cocktail, the Jam and Toast. It may not be enough to spur you to write the next great novel, but at least I can now say, "Don't say I never gave you anything."

JAM *and* TOAST

In the spirit of honoring creativity, we offer you our own twist on the classic French 75, with a delightful pairing of jams and herbs. The herb garnish is forward on your nose, and the rich jam lingers on your tongue. You can switch out and experiment with the flavors as often as you switch lovers (ooh la la). Apricot jam with rosemary, strawberry jam with basil, blackberry jam with mint—get wild. Seek out unique, local homemade jams and seasonal fresh herbs.

SERVES 1

1 oz (30 ml) gin

1 tablespoon jam of your choice

¼ oz (10 ml) lemon juice

2 oz (60 ml) Champagne or sparkling wine

lemon twist, to garnish

herb of your choice, to garnish

In a shaker with ice, combine the gin, jam, and lemon juice. Shake vigorously until everything is blended and the jam dissolves. Pour into a champagne flute and top with Champagne or sparkling wine. Garnish with a lemon twist and your choice of fresh herb.

SYDNEY

~ Australia ~

When you picture Sydney in your mind, you almost certainly envision the Sydney Opera House. The Opera House's stunning white architecture with the Sydney Harbour Bridge in the background has understandably become one of Australia's most recognizable points of interest, and is truly a sight to behold. But there's so much more to Sydney than just the opera house—I mean, when's the last time you went to the opera anyway? Let's be honest, there is little overlap in the Venn diagram of opera enthusiasts and cocktail book readers. Luckily, there's more to Sydney than the Opera House, and more to the Opera House than opera—it's also used for entertainment options like comedy, film, music, dance, and symposiums fill the weekly event calendar.

In a thriving metropolis like Sydney, figuring out how to keep yourself entertained isn't a difficult task. Perhaps the more difficult task is steering clear of all the deadly wildlife. Menacing creatures like the blue-ringed octopus, king brown snake, great white shark, and drop bears seem to lurk around every corner. Tourists seem to be all too aware of these constant threats, yet the Gadigal people (the traditional owners of the land Sydney is on) have been handling it quite well for over 30,000 years and continue to do so.

Australians have more than proven their mettle by merely surviving in a land that is actively trying to kill them. I suppose this constant threat of danger is one of the factors that make Australians so damn fun to be around. The accent alone is reason enough to visit the land down under, but Australians are also celebrated for their friendly and fun-loving vibe. Throw in some beaches, epic surf breaks, and raucous nightlife, and you've got yourself a proper *piss-up*. No worries indeed.

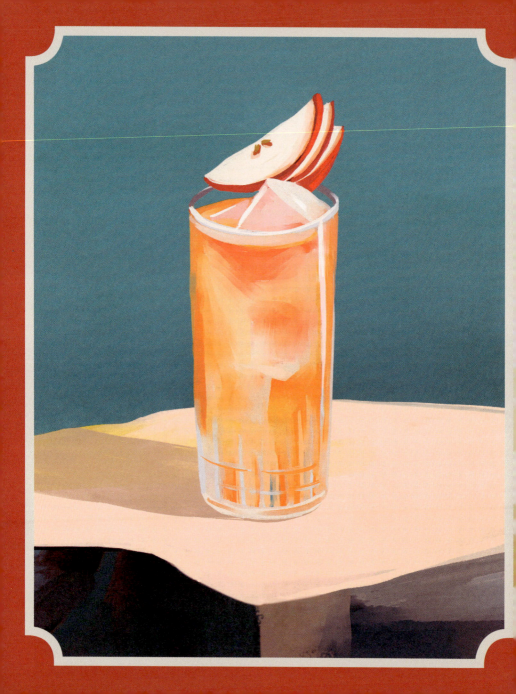

The APPLE FIZZ

This sparkling apple sipper originates in Australia. Story has it, this was invented as a less-boozy version of the Appletini for all the lighter-imbibing Aussies who found the original apple martini taste to be too strong. We have a hard time believing this. Watered-down drinks just mean you can have a few more—take it from the pros.

SERVES 1

1 oz (30 ml) vodka

3 oz (90 ml) apple juice

3–4 apple slices

2 oz (60 ml) lemonade

splash of soda water

Add the vodka, apple juice, two of the apple slices, and lemonade to a cocktail shaker with ice. Shake vigorously. Strain into a highball glass with fresh ice. Top with soda water and garnish with the additional apple slice.

ACKNOWLEDGEMENTS

As much as we love to mix up delicious cocktails on a whim, a fair amount of research and planning went into the creation of this here book. We enlisted the help of all manner of humans: from sommeliers and dive bar owners to world travelers and reclusive sots. Admittedly, our sources are nearly as random as the locations in this book. But that's part of the adventure.

So with that as a preface, we'd like to say a few thank yous to the people who helped us out along our literary pilgrimage.

Clint and Valerie Carr (Loni's parents): Thank you for instilling in me (Loni) your entrepreneurial spirit and hard work ethic. Thanks, Mom, for giving me free rein to experiment with cocktail concoctions, and Dad for teaching me how to hold my liquor like a lady (after *countless* failed attempts). Thanks to both of you for owning and operating a rather legendary small town bar that hosts all kinds of colorful characters who helped fuel my passion for photography and illustration.

Eben Stickney: For his unique and thought-provoking views on the world. Eben's ability to put into words all the thoughts and ideas bouncing around inside his head is truly legendary. Some have described his writing acumen as "adequate" and "good enough" ... and I happen to find these descriptors perfectly suitable. But honestly, Eben has a brilliant mind, and he helped us considerably along our journey. I should probably buy him a drink next time I see him.

Allison Hiew (our editor): For her ability to take my (Brett's) often rambling and incoherent words and make them understandable to the rest of the world. And a HUGE thanks for her endless patience, masterful edits, and brilliant punch-ups.

Hardie Grant (our publisher): For their consideration and willingness to let us create something we are very passionate about. It was always on our bucket list to have a book published, and we are eternally indebted to you for giving us this opportunity.

Bartenders from all across the U.S.: We likely met you while traveling and researching this book. Keith Robins, Meredith Oakes, Anne Killough, and countless others whose names have regrettably slipped from our memory. But you know who you are. Your tips and tricks helped us immensely, and this book was written in your honor.

Patti and Reed Gramse (Brett's parents): The world owes you a huge debt of gratitude for raising such a wonderful, caring, and truly exceptional human. Allowing Brett the flexibility to pursue his wild flights of fancy has likely been demanding at times, but the end result has surely been worth it ... right? Love you both!

Single Barrel Liquor and Bar (Dempsey and Wyatt Hicks): For providing both the Montana "Buzzy Bee" cocktail recipe, and enough lubrication to get us through writing and illustrating this book. Anyone who happens to find themselves in Bozeman, Montana, absolutely MUST stop in to Single Barrel and try some of their amazing cocktails.

The Tallboys Tavern Crew, especially Valerie, Liz, and Kyle: For contributing numerous recipe tips that allowed us to create "everyman" variations of worldly mixology concepts ... and also those delectable boozy pickles!

The Standard Cocktail Bar: Thanks Keith for your recipe suggestions and notes for stocking a home bar ... and for stocking *our* home bar.

Danette Deichmann for providing beautiful travel photography for reference in our Norway illustration, and Rachel Hergett for your worldly advice on travel illustrations.

INDEX

Published in 2022 by Hardie Grant Explore,
an imprint of Hardie Grant Publishing

Hardie Grant Explore (Melbourne)
Wurundjeri Country
Building 1, 658 Church Street
Richmond, Victoria 3121

Hardie Grant Explore (Sydney)
Gadigal Country
Level 7, 45 Jones Street
Ultimo, NSW 2007

www.hardiegrant.com/au/explore

A catalogue record for this
book is available from the
National Library of Australia

Hardie Grant acknowledges the Traditional
Owners of the Country on which we work, the
Wurundjeri people of the Kulin Nation and the
Gadigal people of the Eora Nation, and recognises
their continuing connection to the land, waters
and culture. We pay our respects to their Elders
past and present.

World Cocktail Adventures
ISBN 9781741177954

10 9 8 7 6 5 4 3 2 1

Publisher Melissa Kayser
Project editor Megan Cuthbert
Editor Allison Hiew
Proofreader Lyric Dodson
Editorial assistance Helena Holmgren
Design Erika Budiman, @pixels_and_paper_studio
Typesetting Hannah Schubert
Index Helena Holmgren

Colour reproduction by Hannah Schubert
and Splitting Image Colour Studio

Printed and bound in China by
LEO Paper Products LTD.

The paper this book is printed on
is certified against the Forest
Stewardship Council® Standards
and other sources. FSC® promotes
environmentally responsible, socially
beneficial and economically viable
management of the world's forests.

World COCK TAIL *ADVENTURES*

1. **AMALFI COAST, ITALY** *Limoncello Spritz*
2. **AMARILLO, USA** *The Desert Road*
3. **BARCELONA, SPAIN** *Siesta Para Seis*
4. **BELEM, BRAZIL** *The Sunny Side*
5. **BERLIN, GERMANY** *Essen und Trinken*
6. **BYRON BAY, AUSTRALIA** *First Base on the Beach*
7. **CAIRO, EGYPT** *The Desert Kiss*
8. **CAPE COD, USA** *The Great White*
9. **CAPE TOWN, SOUTH AFRICA** *The Soulmate*
10. **CHIANG MAI, THAILAND** *The Toasted Coconut*
11. **CLARKE QUAY, SINGAPORE** *The Monarch*
12. **CUSCO, PERU** *Blood Orange Pisco Sour*
13. **GALWAY IRELAND** *Hot Apple Toddy*
14. **GEIRANGER, NORWAY** *The Isbjørn*
15. **GOBI DESERT, MONGOLIA** *The Snow Leopard*
16. **ISLE OF SKYE, SCOTLAND** *The Gingersnap*
17. **TEQUILA, MEXICO** *Adios Pantalones*
18. **THE KLONDIKE, YUKON** *The Klondike Sled Dog*
19. **KOLKOTA, INDIA** *The Lucky Lassi*
20. **LONDON, ENGLAND** *The Hooligan*
21. **MEDELLIN, COLUMBIA** *The Drogo Despierto*
22. **MONTREAL, CANADA** *The Hat Trick*
23. **MOSCOW, RUSSIA** *Pochemuchka*
24. **NASHVILLE, USA** *The High Note*
25. **NEW ORLEANS, USA** *The Love Spell*
26. **PARIS, FRANCE** *Jam and Toast*
27. **PORTLAND, USA** *The Pickled Lobster*
28. **QUEENSTOWN, AOTEAROA NEW ZEALAND** *The Kiwi Daredevil*
29. **QUITO, ECUADOR** *Pina Loco*
30. **REYKJAVIK, ICELAND** *Fire and Ice*
31. **SANTA DOMINO, DOMINICAN REPUBLIC** *Mama's Medicine*
32. **SANTORINI, GREECE** *Poseidon's Cup*
33. **SHANGHAI, CHINA** *Coming Up Roses*